JAPAN
the people

Bobbie Kalman

A Bobbie Kalman Book

The Lands, Peoples, and Cultures Series

 Crabtree Publishing Company
www.crabtreebooks.com

The Lands, Peoples, and Cultures Series
Created by Bobbie Kalman
For my good friend Linda Kudo

Author: Bobbie Kalman

Revised edition: Plan B Book Packagers

Coordinating editor: Ellen Rodger

Copy editor: Adrianna Morganelli

Proofreader: Crystal Sikkens

Project coordinator: Robert Walker

Production coordinator: Katherine Kantor

Editors/first edition:
Janine Schaub
Christine Arthurs
Margaret Hoogeveen
Christine McClymont
Jane Lewis

Story on pages 28-29 adapted from *Sadako and the Thousand Paper Cranes* by Eleanor Coerr © 1977, reprinted by permission of G.P. Putnam's Sons.

Photographs:
7122796837/Shutterstock Inc.: p. 13 (top); James B. Adson/Shutterstock Inc.: p. 25 (right); Peter Albrektsen/Shutterstock Inc.: p. 20 (top); Sean O. S. Barley/Shutterstock Inc.: p. 10; Galina Barskaya/Shutterstock Inc.: p. 5 (top left); Aleksander Bochenek/Shutterstock Inc.: p. 21 (bottom); Cristina Ciochina/Shutterstock Inc.: p. 4; Sam DCruz/Shutterstock Inc.: title page, p. 22 (right); Bev Dywan: p. 6; Peter Gordon/Shutterstock Inc.: p. 21 (top); Jarvis Gray/Shutterstock Inc.: p. 24; Naomi Hasegawa/Shutterstock Inc.: p. 11 (left); Alan C. Heison/Shutterstock Inc.: p. 26 (top); Imagemaker/Shutterstock Inc.: p. 26 (bottom); Japonka/Shutterstock Inc.: p. 15; Margus Jukkum: p. 30, 31;

John Launois/Masterfile: p. 11; Michael Ledray/Shutterstock Inc.: p. 25 (left); Andy Lim/Shutterstock Inc.: p.11 (right); Lullabi/Shutterstock Inc.: p. 8 (bottom); Luminouslens/Shutterstock Inc.: p. 13 (bottom); Joan Mann, Cameramann Int'l., Ltd.: p. 3, 7 (inset), 9, 16 (bottom), 18, 19, 22 (left), 23; mfcboy/Shutterstock Inc.: cover; Thomas Nord/Shutterstock Inc.: p. 12; Darko Novakovic/Shutterstock Inc.: p. 27 (bottom); Philadelphia Museum of Art: Given by Mrs. John D. Rockefeller: p. 14; Radu Razvan/Shutterstock Inc.: p. 5 (bottom), 16 (top), 17 (top); Robert Sischy: p. 5 (top right); Tony Stone/Masterfile: p. 27; Asier Villafranca/Shutterstock Inc.: p. 8 (top); Michael S. Yamashita/Corbis: p. 7 (top)

Every effort has been made to obtain the appropriate credit and full copyright clearance for all images in this book. Any oversights or omissions will be corrected in future editions.

Illustrations:
Brenda Clark: p. 28-29
Dianne Eastman: icons
David Wysotski, Allure Illustrations: back cover

Cover: Young Japanese girls, dressed in the popular fashions of Japanese youth.

Title page: Crowds walk through the shopping district, or ward, of Shinjuku, Tokyo, home to the country's busiest train station.

Icon: Paper crane

Back cover: Red-faced Japanese snow monkeys earned their name by surviving in areas with harsh winters.

Library and Archives Canada Cataloguing in Publication

Kalman, Bobbie, 1947-
   Japan, the people / Bobbie Kalman. -- Rev. ed.

(The lands, peoples, and cultures series)
Includes index.
ISBN 978-0-7787-9297-0 (bound).--ISBN 978-0-7787-9665-7 (pbk.)

   1. Japan--Social conditions--1945- --Juvenile literature.
I. Title. II. Series: Lands, peoples, and cultures series

HN723.5.K35 2008   j952   C2008-903483-X

Library of Congress Cataloging-in-Publication Data

Kalman, Bobbie.
   Japan the people / Bobbie Kalman. -- Rev. ed.
      p. cm. -- (The lands, peoples, and cultures series)
   "A Bobbie Kalman book."
   Includes index.
   ISBN-13: 978-0-7787-9665-7 (pbk. : alk. paper)
   ISBN-10: 0-7787-9665-5 (pbk. : alk. paper)
   ISBN-13: 978-0-7787-9297-0 (reinforced library binding : alk. paper)
   ISBN-10: 0-7787-9297-8 (reinforced library binding : alk. paper)
   1. Japan--Social life and customs--Juvenile literature. I. Title. II. Series.

DS822.5.K23 2008
952--dc22
                                                            2008023286

Crabtree Publishing Company
www.crabtreebooks.com   1-800-387-7650

Published in Canada
Crabtree Publishing
616 Welland Ave.
St. Catharines, ON
L2M 5V6

Published in the United States
Crabtree Publishing
PMB16A
350 Fifth Ave., Suite 3308
New York, NY 10118

Published in the United Kingdom
Crabtree Publishing
White Cross Mills
High Town, Lancaster
LA1 4XS

Published in Australia
Crabtree Publishing
386 Mt. Alexander Rd.
Ascot Vale (Melbourne)
VIC 3032

Contents

The people of Japan

Japan is a nation of several islands located along the east coast of China. The people of Japan share thousands of years of traditions and many of the same values. They are bound together by a strong **national pride** in both their **culture** and accomplishments.

Almost everyone in Japan speaks the same language and there are only a few minorities, or groups from a different ethnic background, such as the Ainu or the Ryukuan peoples. The Ryukuan come from the Ryukuan islands, including Okinawa. The Ryukuan people practice different religious traditions, and their language is slightly different from Japanese.

The Ainu live in Hokkaido, the Kuril islands, and Sakhalin. Their language, cultural, and religious traditions are different from Japanese. They are recognized as an **indigenous minority** by the Japanese government.

Japan has one of the world's highest life expectancy rates. Many Japanese can expect to live to age 81. As most of the population is aging, this means that Japan will one day have more elderly people than young people.

The Japanese honor their traditions while adopting the newest trends. This couple, in traditional dress, were just married at a Tokyo shrine.

(above) Families and groups are important in Japanese culture. Here, a group of men and women prepare for an exercise on the streets of Tokyo.

(right) Crowds are common in Japanese cities, but so is courteous behavior!

(below) Three geishas walk through a leafy park on their way to a temple.

The Japanese family

Members of families all over the world feel strong bonds of love and loyalty for one another. Japanese families are no different. There are, however, several characteristics that make Japanese families unique.

The rules of behavior in a Japanese family are strict and traditional. Belonging to an honorable family is a source of great pride for Japanese people. An honorable family member is one who is loyal, responsible, and well behaved. Family members are careful to avoid actions that might embarrass their family.

Smaller families

In the past, Japanese families were much larger than they are today. There were more children, and elderly people often lived with their oldest son and his family. In rural areas, many of these extended families still live together. In cities, however, most apartments are too small to contain big families. Couples have only one or two children, and most grandparents live on their own or in retirement homes.

The keepers of tradition

If grandparents live with their children's family, they share household chores. They help take care of the grandchildren, and instruct them in Japanese traditions. Grandparents in Japan are highly respected for their wisdom.

Japanese mothers

Many Japanese women work until they decide to start a family. After they marry and have children, they often choose to work in the home. A Japanese mother is responsible for looking after the home, budgeting the family income, and supervising the education of her children. Some women go back to working outside the home after their children have passed their important high school examinations. Japan is an expensive place to live, and it is becoming more and more difficult for families to maintain a household on just one salary.

A Japanese father spends some time with his daughters at their favorite park.

Hardworking fathers

Japanese fathers also work hard to support their families. They commute long distances to their jobs and then work long hours. After work, men often go out to dinner with their fellow employees. Japanese companies expect their employees to socialize together. They feel it helps build a strong work-group spirit.

Changing family life

There are many good things about the structure of the Japanese family. Family members try to be supportive and responsible. They feel secure knowing they can depend on one another. Young people show great respect for their parents and elderly relations. Older members of the family demonstrate love and affection for their children and grandchildren.

As in many family situations, however, there are also problems. Fathers have little time to spend with their wives and children, except on Sundays. Some mothers who wish to continue their careers feel frustrated by the limits of their traditional role. Grandparents who live alone often feel lonely and sad.

Honoring ancestors

Japanese people believe that it is important to honor family members who have died. Many families have **Buddhist** altars in their homes dedicated to family **ancestors**. This tradition includes the ancestors in the daily life of the family and ensures that they are not forgotten.

(top) This family shares a meal in their home.

(above) Incense and offerings of fresh food and flowers are regularly placed near photos of the deceased ancestors at the family altar.

Marriage and children

Getting married is an important occasion in the lives of most Japanese people. In the past, parents selected suitable husbands or wives for their children. Today most young people choose their own marriage partners or find an appropriate partner with the help of a professional matchmaker.

A Shinto celebration

Only family members attend the wedding, which is usually conducted by a **Shinto** priest. The most important part is the drinking of the *sake*, or rice wine. The bride and groom drink from three cups, taking three sips from each cup as they say their wedding vows. Both the bride and groom wear traditional **kimonos** for the ceremony, but they often change into **western**-style clothes for the reception. At some weddings, the bride and groom change their outfits three times!

(above) A couple in traditional clothing pose after their wedding.

(right) A wedding procession.

An expensive union

Japanese weddings are expensive. The groom's family pays for the reception because, according to tradition, the bride's parents are giving their daughter to the husband's family. Wedding guests offer generous gifts of money to the bride and groom, but they receive presents from the newlyweds in return. Guests also enjoy a delicious feast.

Starting a family

Japanese couples often wait a few years before starting a family. Today, some couples opt not to have children at all! Most, however, have at least two children. Japanese parents feel that when children are born, they are independent beings who must become familiar with the family group. They carry out many **rituals** to welcome babies and ensure that they feel secure and happy. About a month after birth, babies are dressed in fancy kimonos and taken to a temple to be blessed. Parents offer prayers for the good health of their infants. After the first tooth appears, a baby celebrates his or her first meal. This occasion is the first time the mother feeds her child solid food with chopsticks. On the baby's first birthday, the family holds a banquet to celebrate the day.

Part of the group

In order to make them feel secure, parents keep their children nearby at all times. Babies and young children sleep with their parents until they are four or five years old. They also bathe with their parents. When walking outdoors, a mother carries her baby on her back in a comfortable bag. Parents want their children to feel secure and happy, but they also teach them the rules of family responsibility at an early age. Children learn how to behave politely. They are taught to be honest, to cooperate with other children, and to respect older people.

Work and play

Until the age of six or seven, children have most of their wishes granted. Their parents will do almost anything for them. As soon as children start going to school, however, their carefree lives change. They must study long hours so they can pass difficult exams. Their free time is limited because they have several hours of homework every night.

A mother carries her child on her back in a secure carrier, leaving her arms free.

The family home

The Japanese home is regarded as a private place for family members in which friends are rarely entertained. When entering a Japanese home, every person removes his or her shoes in the entrance hall and puts on house slippers.

Traditional homes

A traditional Japanese house is made of wood. It has one or two stories but no basement. Inside, sliding paper doors called *fusuma* divide the home into separate rooms. These doors can be opened to create one big area. Japanese floors are covered with soft, springy mats called **tatami**. These mats are woven from rice straw and are made to a standard size. They have a sweet, grassy smell when they are new. Rooms are measured by the number of *tatami* it takes to cover the floor.

The dining room

The traditional dining room contains a low table with flat cushions around it. During cool weather, a heater called a *kotatsu* is placed beneath the table. A large, cozy quilt is placed over the table. The quilt holds the heat inside and keeps everyone's legs warm.

Multi-purpose rooms

Japanese rooms contain only a few pieces of furniture, so it is possible to use them in different ways. At bedtime, the living room can be transformed into a bedroom. The table is pushed aside and bedding is brought out of the closet. To make the bed, a foam mattress is laid on the *tatami*. On top of that goes a thin cotton mattress called a **futon**. The sleeper is covered with a softer, fluffier quilt, also called a *futon*.

Japanese homes are kept neat and tidy. Guests are encouraged to take their shoes off and put on house slippers.

A Japanese-style bath

Bathing is a form of relaxation in Japan. Before taking a bath, family members wash outside of the tub to keep the bath water as clean as possible so that all family members can use it. All bathrooms are equipped with drains on their floors. Once the bathers have rinsed off, they get into the square, shoulder-deep tub filled with very hot water. Family bathtubs are usually big enough for at least two people.

Small kitchens

Traditional Japanese kitchens are small. Since fresh food is purchased every day, a small refrigerator has enough room for a day's supply of fish and vegetables. Most meals include rice, so the most important appliance in a Japanese kitchen is an electric rice cooker. A large thermos filled with hot water for tea is kept on most kitchen counters.

Old and new

Western ways have changed many traditional Japanese homes. Modern apartments and houses often have beds instead of *futons*, as well as furniture such as sofas, desks, and dining room sets. But there is usually one *tatami* room as well, kept for special occasions and treasured as a reminder of the old ways. The *tatami* room contains an alcove called *tokonoma*, the place of beauty in the home. Here the family displays an elegant flower arrangement or hangs an antique scroll painting.

(above left) A traditional Japanese shower room with a bucket for rinsing.

(above right) This baby has his own bucket for bathing in.

Rice, noodles, and fish

Japanese people believe that the fresher the food is, the better tasting the dish will be. For this reason they buy their fish, meat, and vegetables at the market each day. Products such as rice, instant noodles, and frozen foods, however, are purchased weekly at local supermarkets.

Japanese people also believe that food should look as good as it tastes. Meals are carefully arranged on pretty ceramic or lacquer dishes to please the eye and whet the appetite. The use of chopsticks is a custom the Japanese share with their Asian neighbors. Japanese chopsticks, called *hashi*, are short and tapered.

A variety of rice

For two thousand years, rice has been the most important part of the Japanese diet. The Japanese have developed many different varieties of rice and countless rice dishes. Rice flour is used to make cookies, cakes, noodles, and crackers. There is a type of tea made from rice and a rice wine called *sake*.

Noodles and more noodles

Japan's most popular fast food is noodles. There are several types, but the two favorite kinds are grey buckwheat noodles called *soba* and thick, white wheat noodles called *udon*. Noodles are usually served in a bowl of fish broth with chopped vegetables. The easiest way to eat a bowl of noodle soup is with a pair of chopsticks!

In Japan, it is not bad manners to make slurping sounds and drink out of the bowl when all the noodles are gone. In summer, noodles are served cold and dipped in a tasty sauce flavored with soya sauce and green onions. Instant noodles are popular because you can have a tasty meal in seconds by adding hot water.

Raman noodle shops are a common site in many Japanese cities. The noodles are a popular fast food.

Seafood lovers

Japanese people eat more seafood than any other people in the world. Fish is fried, steamed, boiled, broiled, and eaten raw. *Sashimi*, thinly sliced raw fish, is dipped in soya sauce. Only the freshest fish is used to make *sushi*, which is slices of raw fish laid on bite-sized blocks of sticky rice. *Sushi* is now popular all over the world. The Japanese also enjoy other types of foods from the sea such as sea urchin, squid, eel, prawns, and seaweed. *Nori* is a type of seaweed that has been dried and pressed into paper-thin sheets. It is used to make rolled *sushi*.

Protein-rich soybean

Soybeans are an important source of protein in Japan. They are made into many kinds of foods such as soya sauce, cooking oil, sweet bean paste that is used in desserts, and soybean curd, called tofu. Deep-fried tofu is served with a ginger-flavored soya sauce. Tofu is also added to soups and stews. Have you ever tried tofu ice cream? It tastes great!

Foods from other places

Even though it is expensive, beef and other meats are now eaten regularly in Japan. Fast foods such as hamburgers, pizza, and fried chicken are also popular. Recently, the Japanese have added milk and other dairy products such as yogurt, cheese, and ice cream to their diets.

Boxed lunches

For Japanese people who must eat on the run, the *bento*, a boxed lunch, is tasty and convenient. A *bento* is divided into sections to hold a variety of foods such as rice, sushi, and pickled vegetables. How a boxed lunch looks is as important as how it tastes, so those who sell *bento* go to a lot of trouble to make them look appealing. *Bento* boxes are made of wood, aluminum, or plastic. They are sold at street stalls and at every train station.

(above) Japanese food is healthy and includes products made from soybeans, rice, and even seaweed!

(below) A plastic sushi display in a restaurant window shows customers the menu.

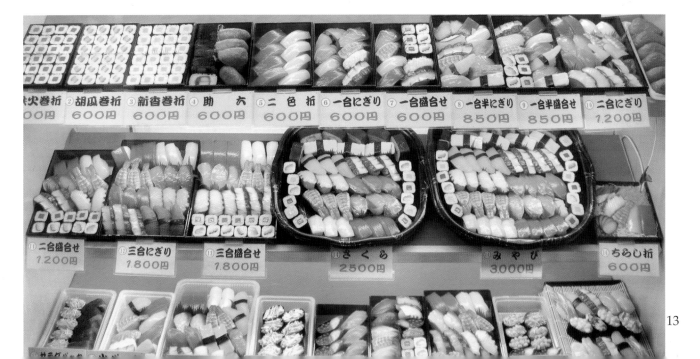

Rules of language

Japanese is a complicated language—both in its spoken and written forms. For example, there are at least five ways to say "I." Greetings are different, too. Every time one person speaks to another, respect must be shown to the older or higher-ranking individual. How deeply a person bows and the words he or she uses changes from one situation to the next. Japanese people always follow strict rules of language to avoid being rude.

Pictures tell the story

Japanese writing is difficult to learn—even for the Japanese! It is a mixture of *kanji* and *kana* characters. *Kanji* are **pictographs**. Each pictograph, or symbol, stands for one word or idea. The characters sometimes look like pictures of the objects they represent. For example, the character for "river" is wavy lines. The *kanji* system of characters was taken from China in the sixth century. Even though the symbols were originally Chinese, the Japanese pronounce them differently.

Kanji characters cannot be sounded out—you either recognize a *kanji* symbol or you don't! High school students are expected to know 1,850 characters by the time they graduate. If you think that is a lot, there are over fifty thousand *kanji* characters in all. Most of these are rarely used, however.

Kana characters

There are two types of **phonetic characters**, called *hiragana* and *katakana*. These characters can be sounded out. Each one represents forty-eight different syllables such as *ka*, *sa*, and *ta*. They were created to write words for which there are no Chinese characters. *Hiragana* are used to write Japanese words, and *katakana* are used to adapt foreign words to the Japanese language. To add to the confusion, Japanese advertising often includes a bit of English or French writing.

Reading up and down

Traditional Japanese is written in columns rather than across a page in rows. A person writing or reading Japanese starts at the upper right corner of the page, moves down to the bottom, and then begins the next column to the left at the top of the page. Not all Japanese books are written in columns, however. Children's books and scientific manuals are printed from left to right and from top to bottom, just as books written in English are. These books open to the left, whereas most Japanese books open to the right. The front of a regular Japanese book looks like the back of an English book.

The art of writing

Writing Japanese can be similar to painting, as each kanji character is like a little picture. A single kanji can be used for one or more words. The meaning of the written kanji depends on its context or location in a sentence. Some kanji have almost a dozen different meanings.

(above) This sign posted next to a volcano uses characters to warn people of the volcano's danger.

(opposite page) The calligrapher in this eighteenth-century woodcut writes with a brush called a fude.

Going to school in Japan is serious business. Once children start kindergarten, their lives quickly begin to change. Students do not always attend neighborhood schools. Their parents try to enroll them in the schools with the best reputations. Young students write tests to compete for positions at these schools.

Hard work

Japanese schools are competitive. Instead of learning at their own pace, Japanese children must all study the same material at the same level. Learning in this way is difficult for some children because not everyone learns in the same way and at the same speed. Students study hard after school and on weekends in order to keep up with their schoolwork. Many go to cram schools where tutors, called "crammers," drill them until they have learned all their lessons. Competition to be accepted to the top high schools pushes students to try to get the highest marks.

A busy school year

In Japan, the school year begins on April 1 and ends on March 31 of the following year. Holidays are in the middle of the school year. Students have so much homework to do that most of them continue to study throughout their summer vacations. School subjects are similar to those studied around the world, such as math, reading, physical education, music, and art. They are also encouraged to take piano, dancing, and other extracurricular lessons after regular school hours.

(top) Students at many Japanese schools wear uniforms.

(right) These children are concentrating on learning their brush strokes.

Air and brush strokes

In the younger grades, a large part of the school day is spent learning to write because students must learn hundreds of *kanji* and *kana* characters. To help themselves memorize the characters, school children trace invisible letters in the air with their fingers. As they get older, students learn the delicate brush strokes of calligraphy.

One exam after another

Writing exams is a regular part of school life. From elementary to high school, children write many difficult exams. The last year of high school is especially hard because the results of these exams determine what universities the students will attend and what kind of jobs they will get. The final high school year is so difficult and stressful that the Japanese have a special name for the experience. They call it "examination hell." Once students are accepted to university, their workload is much lighter.

"Education moms"

Japanese parents, especially mothers, do their best to make sure their children keep up with their schoolwork. For this reason, they are affectionately known as "education moms." Some mothers take courses so they can help their children with their homework. They are also willing to take their children's places in class when the students are ill. During final exam time, many mothers stand in line for hours to register their children for the exams so the students do not have to give up any study time.

These students walk home from school with backpacks loaded with homework.

 # Tetsuo's school day

Tetsuo is eleven years old. He leaves for school at 7:30 each morning wearing his school uniform. He meets three of his friends near his home so they can take the train together. School begins at 8:30. They are excited this morning because their class is going to a museum.

Follow that flag!

Tetsuo's class goes on many field trips each year. Trips are an excellent way to learn history, geography, science, and art. Sometimes there are so many different classes on a trip that the teachers have a hard time keeping track of their students. Young children often wear caps or armbands of the same color indicating the school group to which they belong. Tetsuo and his classmates stay together by following a guide who carries their school flag.

Lunch at school

Tetsuo's class returns to school just in time for lunch! Tetsuo and his classmates eat lunch in their classroom. It is brought from the cafeteria on trays. Today they are having spaghetti and a glass of milk. On other days, the meal is more traditional. It may be rice balls, *sushi*, and pickled vegetables. The students are responsible for cleaning up after lunch is finished.

Classes, chores, and clubs

In the afternoon, physical education is followed by calligraphy class. Tetsuo enjoys learning how to paint *kanji* symbols using a bamboo brush. School is over at 3:20 in the afternoon, but work is not yet finished. It is Tetsuo's turn to help clean up. In Japan, it is up to the students to keep the school clean. Today Tetsuo is raking part of the school yard. On other days he takes photography lessons at his school club. His friends belong to clubs, too. Some play volleyball, and others learn Japanese music.

Plenty of homework

Tetsuo takes the train home and immediately gets out his homework. Today he has about two hours of mathematics and reading to do. Maybe tomorrow evening he will have time to ride his bicycle before it gets too dark. Tetsuo also likes to play baseball with his friends in his free time.

(opposite page) *Tetsuo works on a drawing in his art class.*

(below) *Tetsuo and his schoolmates discuss their notes before taking the train home after school.*

The working world

In the past, the majority of Japanese people were rice farmers. Now most people work in big cities doing all kinds of jobs. Some make manufactured goods or help develop new products. Other people provide services that keep the country running smoothly. Although their jobs may be different, the working habits of modern Japanese people are similar to those of their rice-farming ancestors. Growing rice involved hard labor and long hours in the fields. Farming communities were made up of many families that worked closely together on **communal projects** such as building roads and irrigation canals.

Workplace communities

In some ways, many modern workplaces resemble the old rice-farming communities. People still work closely together on projects, reaching group decisions only after everyone has given his or her opinion. In many offices and factories, Japanese people work side by side, just as they did on farms.

Business suits are Japan's clothing of choice for office wear.

"Let's get to work"

A workday begins with a meeting similar to a **pep rally**. The manager encourages the staff to do a good job. Some companies sing a company song or exercise together before they start the day. At noon, all the employees, including the managers, eat together in the company cafeteria. Throughout the workday, employees feel very much a part of the "company family." Being a good company-family member means working long hours and not taking time off for vacations.

After hours

The company spirit extends beyond working hours. After they leave the office, workers are expected to socialize with clients or fellow employees. The Japanese believe that spending extra time with the members of their work group produces a sense of belonging to the company. Some companies build resorts where employees and their families can spend weekends or vacations.

A job for life

Only the largest, most successful companies can provide their employees with extra perks such as resorts. The large companies are considered good places to work and many people want to work for them. The most successful companies choose their employees from the top universities. University students compete against one another for these high-paying jobs.

Friendly advice

Smaller companies may not provide as much job security, but they still try to create a harmonious company community in the same way that large companies do. Managers offer their workers personal advice and socialize with the staff after work hours.

(right) This man works at the Tsukiji fish market in Tokyo, one of the world's largest fish markets.

(below) Women are often still paid lower wages than men, and many work in service jobs such as these tour guides.

Japanese people are energetic and hard-working. They share a rich cultural heritage, a tradition of close family ties, and a powerful **code of honor**. They also have a strong sense of national identity and work extremely well in groups. All these characteristics have enabled Japan to grow into a strong nation.

The lives of Japanese people have changed rapidly in some ways, but very slowly in others. Some of the problems found in Japan are a result of change, but many exist because not enough change has taken place. Like other countries in the world, Japan needs to examine how it deals with some important issues.

A close-knit society

People who visit from other countries are amazed by the way Japanese people welcome them and treat them with generosity. Showing warmth and **hospitality** to visitors is a matter of national pride for the Japanese. They go out of their way to be helpful to foreigners. Despite this welcoming attitude, foreigners find it extremely difficult to gain acceptance into Japanese society once they become residents.

"Others"

Foreign residents are not the only ones who feel left out of Japanese society. The minority groups of Japan claim they are not treated fairly. These include the original **inhabitants** of the Japanese islands, the Ainu. At one time, these people lived all over Japan in great numbers, but now only about 2,500 are left. Today, the Ainu live in isolated villages in the northern part of the island of Hokkaido. They feel pushed out of Japanese society and excluded from the benefits most Japanese take for granted.

Two or three generations ago, Koreans came to Japan to work as servants. Today, half a million Koreans, many of whom were born in Japan, form a third minority group. These Koreans have never been allowed to become Japanese citizens.

(left) A lot of Japanese women are pursuing professional careers outside of the home.

(right) Japan is a contrast of modern and ancient, and it can be difficult to balance both.

Women in the work force

Although Japanese women are highly trained for careers, many never take jobs outside the home. The traditional role of raising a family and managing a household is still popular, but many Japanese women are becoming less satisfied with their role as homemaker. If women do pursue careers, they are often paid lower wages than men for work of equal value. Some women are eligible for promotions into managerial positions, but few occupy such jobs. The number of women in high positions is slowly increasing, however, just as it is in many countries.

Is the pressure too great?

The Japanese are proud of their system of education. Some people, however, feel that students are under too much pressure. Pupils are expected to memorize large amounts of work, take part in extracurricular activities, and study long hours in the evenings. They also attend cram schools and study during their vacation. Many students, however, are finding it difficult to manage their school workload. In some schools, bullying has become a problem, and many children suffer from *tokokyohi*, or fear of school. To solve these problems, the Japanese government has made a number of changes to the school curriculum.

Burakumin

Japanese people whose ancestors used to work as butchers, leather tanners, and grave diggers are known as *burakumin. Burakumin* means "new citizens." The vegetarian Buddhists of long ago disapproved of the occupations of this group. Although most Japanese now eat meat, the **status** of the two million *burakumin* has not changed. They are still considered lower class no matter what jobs they have or how much money they make. The *burakumin* are discriminated against when they try to find jobs or when they want to marry persons outside their group.

Students in Japan face a tremendous amount of pressure to succeed in school.

Leisure time

Japan has a wide variety of pastimes, from sports and games to festivals. Some of these pastimes are similar to those found all over the world; others are particularly Japanese.

Pachinko

Pachinko is a unique Japanese game. It is similar to pinball except there are no levers and the playing area is upright. *Pachinko* is a game of chance because the player has no control over the metal ball once it has been snapped into play. If the player is lucky, his or her ball will fall into a winning slot and about fifteen balls will come back. The balls can either be played again or traded in for prizes.

Manga mania

Japan is known as a nation of readers. It has the highest literacy rate in the world. The most popular form of Japanese literature is *manga*. Everyone reads these illustrated comic books, from children to adults. At *manga* cafés, customers can read comic books while they enjoy a cup of coffee. You can even visit *manga* museums that feature rare and unusual comics by local artists. Manga began in Japan but has spread all over the world.

(below) Young people play in bands and dress in wacky clothing near Tokyo's Harajuku train station. The area is known for its "Harajuku girls," who dress as characters from animé or manga comics.

Animé

Animé is short for animation. In Japan, a style of animated cartoon featuring Japanese characters with large eyes developed through the 1900s and 2000s. The animated characters were drawn by hand and later with computer assistance. Animé cartoons and stories became popular in books, on television, and as computer games. Today, there are many different kinds of animé, and Japanese style animé has influenced animation throughout the world. People even dress up as their favorite animé characters at shows and events!

Karaoke

Karaoke is a popular pastime in Japan. Up to 20 people can crowd into a karaoke room, called a box, and sing their favorite songs. Older Japanese people sing traditional love songs called *enka*, whereas many young people sing current pop songs. Karaoke boxes are equipped with sofas, coffee tables, and telephones (for ordering snacks) as well as special effects such as flashing lights and disco balls.

(left) A girl dresses up as an animé character at an animation convention.

(above) This man is painting outside in a park.

Outdoor activities

Many Japanese pleasures and pastimes are enjoyed outdoors. In winter, skiing is popular in the northern regions of Japan. At hot spring resorts, bathers soak in steamy pools surrounded by snow and ice. In any season, a visit to one of the country's numerous gardens or parks is another way to enjoy nature. Spring is the season for viewing fruit tree blossoms. In February, the plum trees burst into bloom, and the peach trees follow in early March. Cherry tree blossoms, the most cherished of all, bloom in April. Often, people like to photograph or paint these miracles of nature.

All types of sports are played in Japan. Some are demonstrations of skill and others are made-up games. Some sports have been introduced to Japan from other parts of the world.

Baseball

The Japanese have been playing baseball for over 100 years. It is extremely popular in Japan. Millions of people love to play and watch baseball. Large cities have professional teams, such as the Chunichi Dragons and the Tokyo Giants. Japanese baseball fans look forward to the Japan Series, a Japanese version of the World Series, that takes place every autumn.

Martial arts

Many forms of **martial arts** originated in Japan and have become well known around the world. Two of these are *judo* and *kendo*. Martial arts involve more than just fighting methods. They are disciplines that develop a person's inner strength and control. These arts were practiced and perfected by the *samurai*. Their fighting skills were passed on as sporting activities. Those who practice martial arts know that the techniques must be used only as methods of self-defense. It is more honorable to prevent a fight than to cause one.

(above) Many Japanese people play in amateur baseball leagues in their spare time.

(below) Motorsports, such as motorcycle racing and GT car racing, are popular in Japan.

Sumo wrestling

Sumo wrestling began as a religious ritual hundreds of years ago. It was performed to amuse the Shinto gods. Today, it is Japan's national sport. Six sumo tournaments, each lasting fifteen days, are held every year in Osaka, Tokyo, and other big cities. Millions of fans watch the tournaments on television.

Sumo wrestlers still perform the Shinto traditions that are centuries old. They bow to each other, clap their hands to attract the gods, stamp their feet to drive out evil, and sprinkle salt to purify the wrestling ring. These rituals may take up to four minutes, whereas the actual match may last only twenty to sixty seconds. The object of the match is to force the opponent to the ground or out of the circular ring.

A heavy training program

Wrestlers begin training after completing junior high school. Training involves hard work. Besides learning to fight, sumo apprentices must also clean the training grounds, cook and serve food, and act as servants to the senior wrestlers. Wrestlers gain weight by eating enormous amounts of food at every meal. A large, heavy body is needed for pushing and helps wrestlers stay on their feet during the match. Sumo wrestling careers are short, and only a few wrestlers become rich and famous. Top-ranking wrestlers usually become masters of their own sumo-wrestling schools.

(above) A kendo master with his sword. Kendo means "the way of the sword" and is a traditional Japanese style of fencing that started with the samurai.

(top) Great weight, strength, balance, speed, and mental discipline are all important qualities in sumo wrestling.

27

Sadako and the thousand paper cranes

Sadako gazed out the window at the maple trees swaying in the warm autumn breeze. Her thoughts drifted like leaves in the wind. She sank down in her hospital bed and closed her eyes. Less than a year ago she had been a healthy, fun-loving, eleven-year-old child.

Sadako remembered what a fast runner she had once been. She used to spend every spare moment building up her strength and speed for important races. One day in late autumn, when she was training after school, Sadako suddenly felt very dizzy. She had to stop and take deep breaths. In the following weeks the same feeling returned again and again. Although Sadako felt strong and fit, the dizzy spells frightened her. She told no one about them.

One crisp, cold February day Sadako was running in the schoolyard with her classmates. Suddenly, a frightening sensation in Sadako's head ended the fun. She stopped and breathed deeply, but she could not stop the world from spinning around. Her legs felt weak, and she fell to the ground.

Sadako opened her eyes and looked around the hospital room. "I've been here ever since then," she thought to herself. For eight months Sadako had been in the hospital with **leukemia**. As the months passed, her bones ached, and she grew weaker and weaker. The doctor gave her shots and blood transfusions, but nothing helped make Sadako better.

A gust of warm wind blew in through the window. Above Sadako, 600 paper cranes fluttered in the breeze. Hanging from the ceiling, they looked as if they were flying joyously in a colorful flock above her head. The cranes were of all sizes and colors. Sadako had folded every one of them herself from squares of paper in the ancient Japanese art of *origami*. Everyone who visited her brought a special piece of paper for her to fold into another crane.

The cranes were Sadako's good luck charms. According to an old Japanese legend, the gods would grant the wishes of any person who folded a thousand paper cranes because it was believed that cranes lived for 1,000 years. With every crane she folded, Sadako wished that she would live to be an old, old woman. She also wished for peace in the world. She needed to fold only 400 more paper cranes to have her wishes granted! Sadako made only 44 more cranes. She folded her last one in October of 1955.

Sadako's spirit lives on

In 1945, near the end of World War II, the United States Air Force dropped the world's first atomic bombs on the Japanese cities of Hiroshima and Nagasaki. The tragic effects of these bombs are still being felt by the Japanese people today.

The atomic bombs destroyed two cities and killed over 200,000 people. They also contaminated large areas with radiation, which continues to cause illness and death even today. **Atomic radiation** is dangerous to all living things. It is like a poison that stays inside the body for a long time.

The story on the previous pages is about a real girl from Hiroshima who was two years old when the atom bomb was dropped on her city. Ten years later, she died of a blood disease called leukemia. Her disease was caused by the effects of atomic radiation.

A monument to Sadako

After Sadako's death, her classmates finished folding the rest of the thousand paper cranes for Sadako because they wanted to honor her memory and share in her wish for peace. They also told her story to the people of Japan by publishing the letters she had written to them from her hospital bed. People were so inspired by Sadako's story that in 1958 a monument was built in Hiroshima's Peace Park to honor her and all the children who died because of the bombs. The monument is a statue of Sadako holding a crane in her outstretched hands.

(opposite) Every year, thousands of children visit Sadako's monument and place paper cranes at its base. Individual cranes are strung together with other cranes, forming long, colorful chains.

(right) The Atom Bomb Dome was the only building left standing at the place where the bomb was dropped on Hiroshima. It has been preserved as a reminder of the horrors of atomic warfare.

Praying for peace

Thousands of children fold brightly colored paper cranes and place them under Sadako's monument every year. Millions of paper cranes lie beneath her statue. Each one has been carefully folded by young hands hoping for peace. Each one represents one person's private prayer for a peaceful world. The brightly colored *origami* crane has become a symbol of peace, not only for the children of Japan, but also for people around the world.

Glossary

ancestors People from whom one is descended

atomic radiation Dangerous waves of energy released by an atomic explosion

Buddhist Relating to the religion founded by Buddha, an ancient religious leader from India

calligraphy The art of fine handwriting. In Japan calligraphers use special ink, paper, and brushes

code of honor A set of rules that guides a person in honorable behavior

communal project A task undertaken by a community

culture The customs, beliefs, and arts of a distinct group of people

futon A thin cotton mattress that lies on the floor; a quilt

hospitality Courtesy extended to a guest

incense A substance that produces a sweet-smelling smoke when burned

indigenous Originating or occurring naturally in a particular place

inhabitants People living in a particular region

kimono A loose-fitting, wide-sleeved Japanese robe that is tied with a sash

leukemia A fatal blood disease that can result from exposure to cancer-causing agents such as atomic radiation

martial art A sport that uses fighting techniques for the purposes of self-defense and exercise

minority A small group that differs from the larger group of which it is a part

national pride The feelings of satisfaction that people have about their country

origami The Japanese art of folding paper into objects such as birds and animals

pep rally An event at which a group of people shout and cheer in order to build enthusiasm

phonetic character A written symbol that aids in the pronunciation of words

pictograph A picture used to represent a word

ritual A formal custom in which several steps are faithfully followed

samurai Japanese warriors who lived in ancient times

Shinto The Japanese religion based on the worship of ancestors and the spirits of nature

status Position, rank, or social standing

tatami A standard-sized mat woven from rice straw

tokokyohi A fear of school

western The term used to describe people from the western part of the world, especially Europe and North America, as opposed to people from Asia such as the Chinese and Japanese

Index

Printed in the U.S.A.